THE OPPOSITE
OF
FEAR IS FAITH

Ready, set, go after your dreams!

Joan E. Ruffins

THE OPPOSITE OF FEAR IS FAITH

By Joan E. Ruffins

Printed in the United States of America

Disclaimer. I am not a licensed counselor. All of the content in this book is from my personal experiences. This book is intended as a resource to inspire, motivate and inform you as to how I discovered emotional and spiritual well-being. There are many resources on self-help, this is merely one of many books available to assist you.

Scripture quotations are from the King James Bible. public domain.

First Edition, 2016

Cover Designer: Bozakaric

Published in the United States of America

ISBN: 978-0-99-77298-2-5
ISBN: 978-0-99-77298-1-8

Unfeigned Publishing
Leesburg, FL

For Lawrence,

Your never-ending support on this journey has had the greatest impact. I thank God for allowing you to see in me that which I did not see in myself. I continue to marvel at your unconditional love, patience and strength. Thank God for 20 wonderful years together. You are an inspiration to our family. I love you with all my heart.

CONTENTS

ACKNOWLEDGMENTS

I would like to thank my heavenly Father for doing a great work in me. I can attest with great certainty that His love is the most powerful force in the universe. Thank you for restoring me to my original self. Holy Spirit, I thank you for being my Guide, Encourager, Comforter and Friend.

To my wonderful husband, Lawrence Ruffins, Jr., thank you for sticking with me through thick and thin. Your love has brought restoration and healing. My love for you is boundless. Thank you for your support. Tre, Javon and Lauren, you are my greatest blessings. Your love and encouragement have made a world of difference.

Thank you to my dad and step-mom, Lloyd and Rose Cole for allowing me to see a whole new world. A very special thank you to my father and mother-in law, Pearl and James Lott, Jr., both of you have been a great source of strength. A huge thank you to my father-in law, Lawrence Ruffins, Sr.

Thank you to my brothers and sister, Lawrence Cole, Colin Cole, Andy Smith, Michael Holland, Marlon Holland, Andy Morgan and Ingrid Holland. Each of you have a special place in my heart. A very special thank you to Helen Earle and Leon Solomon. Thank you Mom, grandma Amy, aunt Iris, grandma Kati, aunt Gina and Matilda Sasa for leaving a lasting impression on my heart.

Thank you Pastor Mark Price, it was your call to a greater purpose that propelled me to step out in faith and live life to the fullest. A huge thank you to my friends, co-workers, supervisors and church family in Killeen, especially Dimikki Finley, Simonette Appleton, Linda Pelton, Paula Allen,

Suzanne Nicholas, Amy Kress, Renata Darden, Maureen Adams, Enedina Boggs, Wayne Moore, Karmen Ingraffia, Kristy Wyllie and Tiffany Chaney. It was a joy working and worshipping with you all.

My deepest gratitude to my editing angles, Sonia Matthew, Sherry Mikulastick and Dominique Williamson. Thank you Magdalena Rambally, Gesele Smith, Mildred Bass, Teri Svoboda, Connie Wheeler, Lisandra Rozzi, and Jessica Buerger for your friendship. I appreciate all you have done for our children.

Finally, thank you Aya Fubara Eneli, for challenging me to set a deadline and finish this book. You are an inspiration. I have definitely taken your advice, *Live Your Abundant Life*.

FOREWORD

Joan E. Ruffins is a woman living on purpose and she has thrown out the challenge; go after your dreams! Choose faith over fear.

I have been privileged to know Joan over the last few years. Unbeknown to her, I was drawn to her quiet strength and allure of confidence. The last few months have confirmed everything I sensed about her. This is a woman who has lived and loved deeply, whose had her fair share of tests and trials, and when faced with the crossroad of life that most will eventually experience, she wisely realized that she had a choice and she courageously chose faith over fear.

Her story resonates with me and it will resonate with you too because fourteen years ago, I was at my own crossroads and the pain was so overwhelming and the darkness so enveloping that I briefly considered just giving up entirely on life. But as the famous Christian song says, "Mercy said No." Back then, I sure would have benefitted from a book like this. From the outside looking in, I had it all. I was a young woman with four degrees including a Juris Doctorate from a prestigious university. I had married the man of my dreams and I was confidently and successfully climbing the corporate ladder. An educator, speaker, author and Life coach, I had it all together, till a series of personal tragedies cracked upon a foundation that already suffered from serious faults.

As I read The Opposite of Fear is Faith, every chapter reinforced the struggles I faced, but not only does Joan lay out exactly how fear operates and how it robs us of life, what makes this book stand out is the practical advice she gives for every challenge you may face. For those of us who've had to muddle through our recovery and certainly for those thinking there is no viable path to living on purpose, this book is a God-send.

Be prepared to take a hard and honest look at exactly where you are so you can follow her suggestions for how to reclaim your life, choose faith and not fear and live out your life with purpose. This book is a must read for all who are tired of just merely existing, those who want to support their loved ones who may be struggling with hard things in their lives, and those who want to break through from fear and go for their dreams. Read it and buy a few more copies to hand out to others around you.

Aya Fubara Eneli, MA, JD
Author, Live Your Abundant Life

INTRODUCTION

Your past is not an indication of how high you are able to soar. You have seeds of greatness lying dormant deep down within you. By the time you complete this book, I hope you will discover some important strategies that will help you overcome any type of fears you may be struggling with. It is my hope that you will grab hold of the most potent force in the universe, it has the power to heal and set you free. In fact, it is waiting to assist you right now. I believe you have the ability to overcome your fears, activate your faith and move in the direction of your dreams. Become all you were created to be by harnessing your inner strength. You can visualize the life you desire and speak it into existence.

I battled with PTSD for countless years. After many unsuccessful attempts, I can proclaim today that I have discovered some important tools and strategies that have helped me to overcome this very destructive disorder. I no longer allow the fear it produced to wreak havoc in my mind, heart or life. It took some work but the grip has been released. If you are struggling with fear on any level, there is hope. As long as you have breath in your body, you can overcome and live a fulfilling life. Give yourself permission. You have the power to change the course of your life. Not only do you deserve to enjoy all that is available, but your Creator is waiting for you to fulfill your life's purpose. He takes pleasure when his children live out their destiny. Your greatest years are ahead, live them to the fullest.

SECTION 1

The silent killer

"Fear prevents us from accomplishing our potential and keeps us in bondage."
Aya Fubara Eneli

*F*ear, like carbon monoxide (CO), is colorless, tasteless, formless and odorless. Initially, it is non-irritating and extremely difficult to detect however, it is toxic, poisonous and can be deadly when encountered in concentration. Both fear and carbon monoxide are formed when there is not enough oxygen. Too much inhalation of either can produce poisoning. Chronic exposure of the two can lead to depression, confusion, nausea, repressed memory, heart and respiratory disease, loss of consciousness, suicidal thoughts or send victims into a coma or to an early and untimely death.

Carbon monoxide poisoning is the primary type of poisoning in many countries. According to the Center for Disease Control and Prevention website (2016), "Each year, more than 400 Americans die from unintentional CO poisoning not linked to fires, more than 20,000 visit the emergency room and more than 4,000 are hospitalized." Historically, inhaling too much CO fumes has been used as a common method to commit suicide. Ultimately, fear and carbon monoxide are indistinguishable. Both of these invisible elements possess the ability to take the lives of countless souls.

Carbon monoxide can kill you physically; it can suck the very life out of you as you sleep or go about your daily life. This deadly gas is produced when one burns material containing carbon. There is a greater likelihood of this taking place during cold weather especially, during the winter months, as household fuel-burning appliances or heating systems are utilized more often and when these appliances are not properly ventilated, causing the CO emitted to build up. Some causes include:

- people who use their stoves as a heating source

- anyone that leaves their car running in an enclosed garage

- anyone who uses a charcoal grill indoors

- anyone having anything to do with burning carbon are prone to exposure

Thankfully, carbon monoxide poisoning is preventable. There are numerous ways to avoid such poisoning:

- installing a battery operated CO detector and checking it twice a year

- having your heating system serviced yearly by a qualified technician

- never patching vent pipes with any sticky substances, including duct tape

- avoid using generators in an enclosed area

Simple preventive measures can save a life without much thought or work.

In contrast, fear can kill you emotionally, psychologically, and mentally. This invisible killer has the ability to destroy your dreams, hopes, aspirations and spirit. From the creation of time, fear has overtaken the lives of countless innocent souls. It has sent many to an early grave, robbing them from reaching their greatest potential or fulfilling their dreams. Fear is a silent killer of hopes and dreams. For all practical purposes the fear I am referring to in this chapter stems from my struggle with Post Traumatic Stress Disorder (PTSD). The U. S. Department of Veterans Affairs website (2016), defines posttraumatic stress disorder as, *"a mental health problem that some people develop after experiencing or witnessing a life-threatening event, like combat, a natural disaster, a car accident, or sexual assault."*

Fear is an invisible and silent killer of hopes and dreams. Its poisonous and lethal roots have the ability to extract the very life out of unaware victims. Undoubtedly, fear is real and it holds the ability to paralyze countless victims. This faceless, bodiless, and invisible spirit wreaks havoc on innocent hearts and minds. Examples include:

- nightmares
- depression
- anxiety
- phobias
- isolation
- apprehension
- loss of control
- numbness
- threat

This thing called fear does not discriminate. It cares not about your:

- gender
- race
- national origin
- religious viewpoints
- political affiliation
- sexual orientation

- any other classifications

Fear has the ability to suffocate light and anything that is good. It has no confidence in what is pure or wholesome. Its stench can asphyxiate victims robbing them of air. Indeed, it is controlling, vicious and deadly. It has a stronghold and a consuming presence. In many cases, fear leaves a trail of victims, fighting for dear life. Unfortunately, this thing can reside for months, years, decades or a lifetime:

- It is the opposite of faith.
- It has the ability to hold you captive.
- It attempts to set limits on you.
- It tries to remind you of your past failures.
- It has the ability to hinder you from reaching your greatest potential.

Overcoming fear and living a fulfilling and meaningful life is possible. Forgiveness, restoration and healing are available. Victims possess the ability to grab hold of their lives and live a full and wholesome life.

Where does fear come from?

The tactics fear uses can range from a nicely packaged gift boasting a sophisticated bow of favors or sliding in like a slithery serpent with evil intentions. Fear does not care about its victims only the opportunities they will afford it. Irrespective of the delivery mode, no one is exempt.

Fear has an unlimited amount of entrance points into the human psyche, unsuspectingly entering their hearts or minds subtly and or suddenly. Due to its invisible serpent like nature, it possesses the ability to slitter in without a trace. After it claims its territory fear has the ability to consume its victim without risk of detection and eventually reign supreme freely. Fear and carbon monoxide operate on a similar wave length and they are both undetectable menaces.

Fear is the human race's greatest enemy, it has the ability to steal your joy, kill your faith and even destroy your dreams. At any given moment, fear has the ability to intrude and dominate its victims. Here are a few examples that will expose fear:

- A physically abused child or adult may blame themselves. Whether they were victims of rape, molestation or incest they may conclude that the abuse is somehow their fault (self-blame).

- A physically or verbally abused victim may feel there is no way out of an abusive relationship hence, (fear of physical harm or death).

- An emotionally disabled person living with conditions such as Autism, Parkinson, Asperger, Bipolar, ADHD, PTSD, OCD, Bipolar, depression or Schizophrenia, may feel they brought the condition on themselves (mental, physical and or emotional difference).

- Fear of being hurt may reside in the heart of the neglected, divorced, separated or abandoned person.

- "You are incapable of being loved or loving again," may whisper in their ears (relationship isolation).

- Fear of never being satisfied, losing one's position or possessions, aging, and loss of mental ability can be dreadfully terrorizing plus the thought of dying may consume the heart of the unsatisfied (fear of loss or demise).

- Fear of not having enough money, friends or the latest gadget may consume the heart or mind of victims (being unfulfilled).

- Fear of failure may reside constantly in the person that lacks self-confidence (insufficiency).

- Fear of_____may consume you on a daily basis.

There are countless other reasons why fear may slip in and live in the heart and mind of people around the world.

Feelings from fear

Fear dismantles its victims on every side. There are often feelings of unworthiness and uselessness. Emptiness, loneliness, depression, hatred, thoughts of suicide, and all sorts of ill intentions are always on the prowl when fear is present. Most victims often work overtime in order to mask their fears. Some things that may run through their minds without much thought include:

- looser
- failure
- self-blame
- self-hatred
- worthlessness
- good for nothingness
- you'll never amount to anything
- hopelessness
- abandonment
- helplessness
- shame
- disgust
- uselessness
- disgrace
- doomed
- destroyed
- unworthy
- unacceptable
- untrustworthy
- darkness

Victims may not seek or receive support from family, friends or health care professionals due to various reasoning such as:

- fear of judgment
- fear of ridicule
- fear of abandonment
- fear of being labeled
- fear of being discriminated
- fear of being betrayed

Fear of being disassociated from family, friends, and coworkers generally ranks as the primary reason victims may not open up or share their experiences and feelings.

Is fear self-inflicted?

Some may argue that fear is self-induced or non-existent, claiming you brought it on yourself or it's all in your head. I beg to differ. No sane person wholeheartedly opens their heart or mind and welcomes this thing into their life. A person's perception is their reality. Fear can take root at any given moment due to one's upbringing, environment, past or present negative experiences, or any other trigger that interferes in one's daily function in life. This debilitating fear can result from:

- abuse
- rape
- incest
- assault
- abandonment
- war
- divorce
- any mental or emotional disorder

The primary fear

My objective is to focus on the fear that has hindered people from pursuing their dreams. The graveyard, the richest place on planet earth is full of countless unfulfilled and unrealized dreams, goals and aspirations. Buried alive and completely useless are many possible world changing and life-altering ideas that have been locked away in an unrecoverable black box of dream killing fear. If the graves could release their secrets they would reveal many inventions that had the possibility to change the course of history by improving life on earth, cure deadly diseases, or a discovery of ways to improve our planet. The possibilities within the gravesites were endless.

The inability to go after one's dreams has kept countless people bound for years. The person desiring to accomplish great things may feel as though he or she does not possess the ability to leap forward and stride into his or her destiny. As you may already know too intimately, many negative feelings attach themselves to fear and can be difficult to remove. Indeed, the heart and mind of victims are forever changed when they make contact with fear. I can attest from experience that accomplishing your dreams may appear like a far-fetched or distant fantasy. However, by releasing your preconceived notions and fears, you have the power to change the course of your life. In order to reverse the damage, a drastic agent of change must come in and perform a complex operation. Doing so, will free victims all over the world. Infusing your heart and mind with love will not only open new doors, but it will drive out your fears.

Overcoming fear

Overcoming fear can be a continual struggle, however it is possible. In order to return to a level of normalcy, each victim has to identify the best mechanisms, techniques or strategies that work for his or her needs. Regardless of the chosen path, with the right tools and support, I believe all victims are equipped with the ability to push through to the other side and overcome their fears.

Recalling, replaying and looking at the root cause may make you feel uncomfortable, however, you have to dig deep down to the root and revisit the dark and wretched places in your mind to get to the bottom of it all. The pain may seem too vivid, causing you to try and abandon ship. Don't quit now, this is a vital turning point. Get to the core, do it quickly, shed light on the secrets and you will not have to keep returning to that place in your mind. Exposing fear will lift it off your shoulders and lighten the load you have been carrying around.

At first, it may seem difficult to speak of the horrific things you may have experienced, but it is imperative that you do. There are many opportunities to shed light on the fear that has tried to cripple and hold you captive. Many knowledgeable and concerned individuals are available to help take the load of fear off your shoulders. Simply articulating or putting your experiences or feelings into words can begin the healing process. It is extremely satisfying to know that information is readily available simply by conducting a quick search on the internet. You will discover a plethora of ways to overcome your fears including:

- Recognizing the root cause
- Utilizing various breathing techniques
- Meditating
- Having a positive attitude
- Seeking professional help

For me, healing began within. As a result, I have discovered the most essential element extended from the Creator to man. This gift has helped me to crush my fears and overcome them victoriously. This wonderful discovery has stood the test of time. It is pure, flawless, and eternal. It possesses the power to heal, restore and renew on all levels.

I am well aware that the past is the past and it cannot be changed. The memories and images from the incidents that produced fear will by no means evaporate magically. However, I am suggesting you abandon your fears by replacing your past hurt, pain, abuse, neglect, mistreatment or anything else you may have endured with this wonderful thing I am recommending. It cannot be bought in stores or online. I believe it will help you overcome your fears, go after your dreams and live the life you desire. In order to get the full effect of this unique gift, we merely need to take the time to recognize, unlock and utilize it. My hope for you is that you too will rediscover this powerful gift and allow it to transform you from the inside out. Let me try to give you a clear picture of how I overcame this horrible thing called fear.

For years, I struggled with fear, unsure of where it emanated from until I had an epiphany. After serving in the military, I had no clue I would carry around such heavy baggage on my shoulders. I was under the impression, after I removed my green and black camouflage basic duty uniform (BDUs), black combat boots, insignias and headgear, everything would return to normal. Needless to say, some 17 plus years after I laid down my duffle bag, M-16 rifle, and bayonet, things refused to return to the normalcy I knew prior to my enlistment in the United States Army.

After acclimating myself back into the civilian way of life, I felt out of place, akin to an alien in someone else's homeland. I carried around a dark secret that was hidden in hopes that no one would discover the battle I was fighting on a daily basis. Internally, I was spiraling out of control, even though everything appeared normal on the surface. I was not only meaner than a junk yard dog and snappy, but I taunted with negative thoughts, anxious, irritable, ravished with nightmares, but I also struggled with concentration and isolation from people, places and certain things. I battled with a slew of other unhealthy stressors as well.

At work I, succeeded at functioning as normal as I could, accomplishing the goals and missions of the organizations that placed their confidence in me. I enjoyed helping to mold the next generation by fulfilling my childhood dream of becoming a teacher. Even though, as a child fantasizing about teaching, I did not foresee the struggles I would battle with, internally. With that being said, I did the best I could to control my internal struggles and endured through the school years.

My private life was a vast contrast, at home I was a different individual; not only was I numb, cold, and inattentive, but I was standoffish and unaffectionate. I was not the wife or mother I envisioned when I was planning my life as a teenager. I was no way close to the loving, affectionate or understanding wife my husband deserved, nor was I the caring, compassionate, patient, kind or fun loving mother our children needed. I was there but I really wasn't there. It was as if I was simply existing rather than living.

At times I felt like a rock, a body without a heart or mind of my own. I found little pleasure in things I once enjoyed, my energy level was constantly hovering in the negative and it was as if my mind was always bombarded with unnecessary stuff. I often wondered: who suffered most. I'm sure my husband and three children experienced a greater hardship than I did. Indeed, they did not deserve to be treated so callously. I wish I could have taken back all the harsh words and cold feelings I displayed towards them. Even though I was surrounded by a loving family and living in a beautiful house, I felt scared and empty on the inside, like the world was caving in on me. The battle was in my mind, but my thoughts were manifested into actions. The fears of this world had clouded my mind and judgement. After acknowledging how my negative behaviors were affecting my family as well as my work life, I made a conscious effort to change the person I had become. However, after many failed attempts, I came to my wits end.

I swallowed my pride and marched right into the Veteran's Hospital (VA) and informed my doctor that I needed something because I felt as if I was coiling out of control. I enlightened her that I had weird sentiments running through my head, and that I believed I had Attention Deficit Hyperactivity Disorder (ADHD). On the contrary, it was in fact, Post-Traumatic Stress Disorder (PTSD). Not wanting to jump to any conclusion based on one person's opinion, I went to speak with two additional specialists.

They confirmed the diagnosis. Immediately, I dispelled the notion, explaining there's no way I can afford to carry that stigma around. I continued stating there was no way a person like me could have PTSD since I was not deployed to an active war zone. Noting that I did serve overseas, but did not think for a second there was a correlation with the two. At that time, I was unaware that PTSD was no respecter of person. As I continued speaking with the doctor, we delved a little deeper going as far back as my childhood and realized there were incidents from it that contributed to the fear I had been struggling with. That was the first and last time I revealed what was taking place in the battlefield of my mind to someone other than my husband. I felt this great relief come over me after letting the cat out of the bag.

Prior, I was probably one of the world's greatest pessimists, always seeing the glass half empty however, my husband remained strong and optimistic for me during my entire ordeal. Without his support, encouragement, understanding, patience, and unconditional love I quite possibly may have self-destructed. Finally, I yielded the relief I was seeking.

God healed me by reaching down to the dark, fear infested parts of my being with the love he imparted to my husband. His love revitalized the dark, dry and corroded places. Reflecting, I can attest with great certainty that God's unconditional love imparted to me by way of my husband was the primary factor to my healing. It was infectious; I allowed it to saturate my whole being. When it had taken root the nightmares, depression, anxiety, isolation, loss of control, numbness, and other fears began to melt away like snow on a sunny day. I witnessed first-hand the power of love, God's pure and unblemished love working on the inside. I felt like I was revived like a vampire. The love was the blood and I drank it daily. This solidified that love is more powerful than hate, hurt, anger, rage, pain, the past or any fears.

Transforming back to my original self was not a walk in the park. There were many instances when my fears tried to supersede love, however, after embodying my humanness I realized it was worth fighting for. It was with a made up mind that I continue to live a victorious life free of fear. I can attest that pure undefiled and perfect love makes the difference. It possesses the ability to heal, restore and set free that which is broken, cold, hurt, abused, damaged or lost. Love is the key, love is real and love is necessary. I have a greater appreciation for the scripture, *"Two are better than one."* Plain and simple, we need people.

Perfect love deletes all fear

Love from above is powerful and possesses the ability to accomplish great things the world over. It is the most recognizable word and symbol in our galaxy. Regardless of where we are located, irrespective of the language barriers, love has the ability to unite us. It can cover past hurts, pains, failures and fears. It is a healer, having restored countless damaged, neglected, abused and forsaken hearts and minds. If you have not put it to the test I challenge you to give it a try. Allow love to heal, renew, restore and rejuvenate the inner most part of your being. My hope is that you will discover a whole new world with new beginnings. The universe is waiting to embrace you with its arms wide open. There is so much more to gain when you open your heart to perfect love.

Why choose love as a healing mechanism?

God is love. We were created by love to love, because we are a product or our Creator. Since his nature is love so is ours. Regardless of your circumstance, know with great certainty that you are loved. There are zero restrictions on unconditional love. Love is the ultimate healer, the answer to most, if not all of life's problems. Take a few moments and allow the idea of love to saturate your heart and mind. Truth be told, it already belongs to you. Taste it, embrace it and allow it to take root in your heart and mind.

You deserve to use it liberally and without reservations. Embrace yourself with this all-consuming, pure and undefiled love from above. You hold the keys to your healing and your destiny, the one master key that will open both doors is love. Here are a few keys:

- Acknowledge that God is love
- Receive His love
- Build a relationship with God through:
- Praying
- Meditating
- Fasting

Help someone

Victims of fear will generally open up when there is trust and respect. They will come clean if and when they feel comfortable with the people they share their darkest secrets with. Trustworthiness and confidentiality are the main ingredients that will cause victims to invite outsiders into their world.

Be a supporter

A supporter is a person who supports someone in need. If you are not a victim of fear, there is so much you can do to help. If you suspect someone is struggling with any type of abuse, disorder or disease, please reach out and help. Something as simple as a listening ear or a warm embrace can make a world of difference. Be open, understanding, compassionate and empathic. No need to say, "I know how you feel" or other cliché.

The fact of the matter is, unless you have experienced what a victim has been through you will not truly be able to comprehend the depth of the hurt, pain or abuse. As a supporter you have an obligation to society. I implore you to lend a helping hand. Don't be bashful and don't hold back your love or support. In many cases, it may make a huge difference to a victim of fear. In fact, you may even save a life.

Destination contentment

Whether in our private or professional life, we are all on a quest to arrive at that magnificent place called contentment. It isn't as unattainable or as far-fetched as one may think. The fact of the matter is; this destination is around the corner of a four letter action word called *work*. It has taken men to the moon, built great coliseums, pyramids, walls, castles, monuments, mansions and nations and brought inner peace to many. I have discovered this place of contentment not by traveling around the world but by looking within daily. Here are a few strategies I have incorporated into my lifestyle that have helped me live the life I desire.

- Forgive yourself--forgiveness is for you not your offender. You deserve to be healed, renewed and restored.

- Unlock your inner self:

  1. Praying--connects you to your Creator
  2. Meditating--connects you to your Spirit man

3. Fasting-connects you to your true self

- Create a plan of action--visualize the future you desire and set a completion deadline. Find an accountability partner who has your best interest at heart, someone who will hold you accountable, encourage and help you along your journey. That partner can help propel you to higher heights and a deeper depth, so choose wisely.

- Embrace your newness- where you are standing or sitting this very moment is the perfect place to begin. The time is right. Begin to grab hold of your life. The future you desire is attainable. You hold within your hands and mind the abilities to cause your dreams to come to fruition. Regardless of the size, the world awaits your gifts and talents. Not only are you wanted but you are needed in this life and at this present moment. Decide in your mind and heart to go forth and fulfill your life's purpose. Abandon your past, embrace your present and focus on your future. Know that you have everything you need to succeed and win in this race called life. Go after your dreams and live the life you deserve.

Intimate acquaintances

Spending a number of years under the ever constant threat of fear gave me an intimate look into a world filled with negative energy. There was little physical evidence, however, the cognitive and psychological hold it had on me was insurmountable. Dark clouds hovered atop appearing like a companion, accompanying me to and fro, day in and day out. Not only did I bathed and dined but I also slept with my fears.

There was little room to escape; being that every crease and crevice was filled with poison. For instance, after receiving the idea to write this book, I dispelled the notion primarily due to my introverted personality. I swept the thought under the rug for over 10 years formulating an endless list of invalid reasons why I couldn't write a book. I knew fear would have won if I did not take the necessary steps and move forward and accomplish the dream I had lying dormant for so long.

Know your worth

Take a glimpse at the reflection in the mirror. You are beautiful, handsome, intelligent, worthy, strong, hopeful and full of love. Speak to yourself. Build up your self-confidence. You have all the power you need to succeed. You are made in the image and likeness of your Creator, therefore you possess His attributes. Since He is love, then you are love. Since He is peace, happiness, joy and everything that is good then so are you. You are equipped with the power to accomplish all you hope to achieve.

Take a moment and declare to yourself:

- I am love
- I am worthy
- I am well
- I am healed
- I am whole
- I am happy
- I am forgiven
- I am peaceful

- I am content
- I am powerful
- I am beautiful
- I am hopeful
- I am abandoning my past
- I am forward looking
- I am fulfilling my destiny
- I am fearless
- I am faithful
- I am friendly
- I am content
- I am love
- I am_____
- I am_____
- I am_____
- I am_____
- I am_____
- I am_____
- I am_____

The best teacher

I am thankful to God, not for the horrific experiences I went through, rather for the opportunities to experience firsthand what so many in the world over have endured. I would never wish the negative feelings, thoughts, nightmares, restlessness, inattention, or any other fears on anyone else. My hope for everyone is to use the past as an experience, as a great teacher, to learn from it and to use it to help or heal someone that may be struggling at this very moment. James 1:2-3 states,

"Count it all joy when ye fall into divers temptations, knowing that the trying of your faith worketh patience." I can definitely agree with him, the difficulties or challenges we are presented with are not to destroy us; rather they are to build our character and cause us to grow. It is through much hurt or pain that we can triumph victoriously and proclaim, "I am a survivor and not a victim." Love is the greatest healer; in addition, I would add forgiveness, time, and a change in mindset to my list.

Your future is very bright

Walk boldly down the path into your newly discovered strength. Know that you are stronger and wiser than you may think. Take the time to rediscover your true self. Know for certain that you are:

- gifted
- talented
- intelligent
- full of life
- full of love
- full of hope

You are bold and extremely valuable. Once you have a made up mind, there is nothing you cannot accomplish. Adopting a new mindset and continuously reminding yourself of how far you have made it will cause you to revamp your outlook on life. Be certain that you are well capable of accomplishing what you desire. Allow nothing to hinder or divert you from walking into your new purpose. With a made up mind, focus and determination you are destined for greatness. You have been equipped with the tools necessary to succeed so use them wisely.

My invitation

Your past does not define you; simply use it as a teacher. Let it elevate you to a higher level. Know with great certainty that you are a survivor and not a victim. Disrobe your soiled garments, cleanse yourself with love, adorn your body with the sweet fragrance of hope, dawn your new attire, and allow it to embody you. You are:

- valuable
- unique
- worth much more than fine gems

SECTION 2

Faith

"Hopes are thoughts in your imagination that you can change into present day facts".
Dr. Wayne Dyer

*T*he opposite of fear is faith. Similar to fear, faith is unseen to the naked eyes. Neither can be touched, tasted, or smelled. Both operate in the supernatural realm. If you say you believe in God, the Creator, the Universe, the Supreme Being, Allah, Brahma, or any other deity; you profess having faith in that unseen Spirit. Consider this; it takes faith to have faith in things outside the physical realm. In the first book of the Bible Moses states, *"In the beginning, God created the heaven and the earth."* The Creator created. However, before creation took place more than likely the Creator had in mind the end result of what He expected. It is fair to assume that He visualized the outcome he desired before it came into existence.

After creating the world, He proclaimed, *"Let there be light."* In fact, after speaking light into existence there were a number of additional "let there be", describing the blueprint of how our world came about. The firmament, waters, dryland and finally man came forth from the speech spoken by the Creator. What a powerful example of faith. The author continued discussing how the Creator created the heavens, earth, living creatures, male and female in his own imagine.

After God completed his work, He was not only pleased with his creation; but He gave them specific instruction, exclaiming how they should be fruitful, multiply, replenish, subdue and have dominion over all the earth. What a terrific proof of how God had faith in Himself by speaking creation into existence thereby, moving His words from the supernatural to the physical realm.

This will come as no surprise to you that faith is the product of everything you see with your eyes, all which is touchable, and anything you can taste. Not only does God require us to have faith in Him; He expects us to accompany our faith with action. Faith is just an idea unless you add some work to it. James 2:17 supports this notion, *"Even so faith, if it hath not works, is dead, being alone."*

In order to be effective, you must put into practice that which you hold true. Whatever you desire to accomplish starts within. Since everything begins as an idea, visualizing that which you hope to accomplish must be accompanied with an action. First come faith, then hope, then action. Faith is from God, and it is a belief in a future expectation. Similar to how God called this universe into existence, you too possess the ability to create the future you desire. Whatever you think in your heart or mind that is what you are and will continue to become.

- Whatever you feed your conscious mind that thing will produce the most fruits.

- Whatever you desire or invite into your life will come to pass if you believe and work at it.

- Train yourself to become cognizant of your words but most of all guard your thoughts.

Not just another five letter word

Faith is so much more than a belief in the unseen; it is not merely just another five-letter word that should be tossed to and fro. There are various meanings to this life changing word.

At this time, I will focus on faith as a way of thinking and living. Living in faith is living an optimistic life, one where you see the glass half full as opposed to half empty. Not only is it having a positive attitude, but faith equates to living a life filled with belief in the unknown. Regardless of how you utilize the word, it is powerful and effective when executed with an open mind. Faith is imperative to living a full life; however, it is of null effect if it is not combined with works.

Hard work will always pay off in the end, therefore, taking action means you not only have an intention, but you are taking that intention one step further and acting upon it. In order for your faith to become a reality, you have to speak what you desire into existence. When you exercise your faith, you have the right to expect that which you place in your mind to materialize. *Having faith, a belief in yourself and abilities is the first step in realizing your destiny and walking into it.* Come to think of it, in my earlier years I was under the impression that only certain people's faith worked and yielded a return. I often marveled at how amazing it would be to be a part of such an elite group of selected people, little did I know that the universe cares not about your:

- gender
- education
- finance
- religion
- race
- background
- status
- titles
- labels

**Bottom line, faith works if you work your faith.

All too often we create these preconceived notions that only exist in our heads. We all ought to grab hold of this universal truth that our Creator is ready, willing and able to assist us in all of our undertakings. He cares deeply for all of His creation since he fashioned, molded and shaped us in his imagine and likeness. We simply need to let our request be made known. Whatever you are desiring, speak the words and they will come to fruition.

- Speak the life you desire into existence.
- Take action.
- Remind yourself of your goals.

Speak in the present tense by stating you are what you are hoping to become or hoping to obtain, such as:

- I am smart.
- I am happy.
- I am love.
- I am peace.
- I am living my dream.
- Watch it manifest itself.

By far one, of the greatest examples of faith would have to be a parable in which Jesus told his disciples, *"If ye had faith as a grain of mustard seed, ye might say unto this sycamine tree, be thou plucked up by the root, and be thou planted in the sea; and it should obey you."* Looking back during the dark and uncertain period of my life while struggling with PTSD; I can only imagine what I could have done to overcome my struggles, if I had truly grabbed hold of this thing called faith. Had I been aware of this life changing tool, I probably would have made more progress sooner rather than later. Needless to say, I am extremely thankful I had the unique opportunity to experience the struggle countless souls endure. Because I have this unique perspective, I hope to inspire others to never give up on their future. Help is available; faith is an individual tool that has the ability to assist you along the way. However, you must be truly convinced that faith takes work in order to be truly effective.

Future

Faith is speaking into your future. Since faith called this universe into existence, we are assured that we possess the power and ability to shape the future we desire. Since faith is no respecter of persons, you too are able to have what you desire and speak it into your life.

Yes, it takes faith to move mountains, but you have to start chipping at the mountain little by little. You should not think it strange when you hope to achieve something greater than your level of faith. Give your faith a test drive, nothing wrong with starting small and gradually progressing as you grow and strengthen your trust and confidence in your higher power.

Faith is a futuristic word since it is solely based on a future expectation. This verb, an action word requires not only simply believing, but it also requires work in order for it to be realized. Once again, you must take action in order for your faith to work. Faith is belief in the supernatural or an unseen spirit waiting to assist and propel you into your destiny. Activate your faith by doing something.

Faith is not only confidence in the future, but it possesses the ability to help you accomplish your dreams and goals. However, if you continue to do the same thing expecting a different result you are fooling yourself. Yes, fear has hindered many including yours truly.

Confidence is an attribute of faith. For example, walking confidently into a dark room and believing no harm will befall you. So it is similar to walking boldly into uncharted waters with great certainty that every step you take will lead straight down the right path.

Seed

Faith is a seed. When watered, cultivated and allowed ample time it will grow exponentially. Since faith moves God, it may be fair to say that the more you utilize it the more it will grow and the greater the rate of return you are likely to yield.

Faith can propel or boost you into realizing your dreams. Similar to a muscle that is worked out at a gym on a regular basis, so too your faith will grow when you begin to exercise it.

The scriptures plainly explain, *"Without faith it's impossible to please God."* He requires us to have faith in Him. We can't say we love God and believe in Him without faith.

Focus and determination when combined with faith will assist you in realizing your dreams and goals. Since everything you see with the naked eyes is a product of faith, it may be fair to assume that faith must be the foundation to achieving your dreams and goals. Your Creator, God, the Universe, the Most

High, Allah, the Light is waiting to assist and guide you. He is patiently waiting to accompany you, He desires to assist you and He wants to take part in helping you accomplish your goals, dreams, visions and aspirations.

Faith is belief in the unseen. If you say you believe in God, you are utilizing faith because you have never seen God. Therefore, faith is a belief system that possesses numerous elements. Let me explain. Faith by itself is of null effect until works is involved. Day in and day out, we utilize our faith without much thought.

- By faith, we accept a new job
- By faith, we relocate
- By faith, we get married
- By faith, we have children
- By faith, we raise our children
- By faith, we purchase a house
- By faith, we purchase a vehicle
- By faith, we purchase everything necessary for living
- By faith, we live life
- By faith, we dream
- By faith, we hope

Faith is such a powerful word grab hold of it. You will be amazed by all the awesome things you will discover when you realize how faith truly works.

Faith is an awesome virtue. It can help you set the course for the rest of your life. Indeed, it is so much more than hope in the future. It's a way of life for those who recognize and decide to live life unconventionally. All too often we get accustomed to the daily nine to five grind, daydreaming of what life could be. Many of us never take the necessary steps needed to venture down the road less traveled. On the other hand, people who take the leap of faith and leave their comfortable jobs and dare to step in uncharted water, not only stretch their faith but they usually discover that the only thing that separated fear and faith was a very thin line. For sure it is much easier to do nothing and remain stagnant. Simple math proves:

- Nothing from nothing equals nothing, 0-0=0.
- Something from nothing equals nothing, 0-1=0.
- Nothing from something equals something, 1-0=1.

Bottom line, do nothing and nothing will get done. Do something and something will get done. Faith is taking nothing and adding, something which equates to something. Add faith to whatever you have and watch how it grows, multiplies and bears countless fruits.

Because faith was the foundation that brought this world into existence, there should be little argument if I say faith is the foundation to realizing and accomplishing your dreams. Irrespective of the size, we have the power to speak to any situation in our lives. This solidifies the fact that we are born with the power to unlock and utilize our faith. Faith grows when we put it to work. For many of us, our faith is simply hanging out dormant waiting to be exercised, activated or challenged. Remember faith is internal. It can't be bought or sold. We are all born with a specific measure of faith, how we use it is entirely up to us.

I suggest you use your faith constantly by speaking those things that are not in the physical realm as though they already exist. As in life or any endeavor, you have to get to work in order to yield a product. The fruits of your labor will come to fruition when you actually labor, meaning after you get to work. Indeed, action speaks louder than words.

Regardless of how huge or small your dreams are it takes faith to attain the reality you hope for. It takes faith to believe in the supernatural. Since no one has seen God and lived, I want to stress, it takes faith to believe in an invisible God.

If you say you love God, your faith has been made perfect when you love unconditionally. Perfect love equates to loving not just your friends, family, neighbors, coworkers, and people you are fond of, but in addition, you are expected to love your enemies as well as the unlovable. Faith is so much more than meets the eyes. Utilizing this tool will not only assist you in fulfilling your life's purpose, it will help you exercise love and hope for someone else. Faith can take you from one realm to the next without any need to travel.

Focus on your future. Give full attention, focus and energy to your future. Stop draining your energy on your past. When you place your focus on something you are giving full attention to that thing. I believe your future is so important that I need you to take the time now and do what is necessary to prepare for it. Participate in your future, better yet take control of it; because quite frankly, your future begins right now. **Now is the acceptable time to crush your fears, activate your faith and go after your dreams.** They may just be one in the same.

Faith is forward looking. The past is depleted energy, don't waste your time or energy recalling past hurts, mistakes, disappointments or failures. Realize the future is not some distant futuristic eon, it is now. The choices you make this instant will no doubt affect your future. Whether you choose to act or not will determine your outcome. Faith is a shield; you need to put it on for protection from future doubts and fears. It will carry you through your toughest times. Faith is certainty of a greater outcome. It is your shield of protection in times of fear, doubt and uncertainties.

While serving in the military, I underwent an enormous amount of training. This was in preparation to defend myself, squad, company, battalion, post, and country as a whole. I was trained with various tools, and weapons needed to succeed in the event there was an attack against the government I pledged my allegiance to regardless if it was a domestic or foreign attack. In the event that I was to deploy to a war zone my combat boots, m16 rifle, bayonet, launchers, miles gear, gas mask and everything else I needed gave me confidence that I could fight and come out victoriously. I was truly content with the physical tools I received however; I was more than content that I had faith since it was the most important weapon needed in my tool kit.

Faith is protection, a prerequisite before stepping into battle. Before you start your new journey, grab hold of faith, it will be necessary. Faith in your Creator, the Almighty, a Higher Being is necessary. It will help you navigate this life successfully. Faith is vital, crucial, and imperative in this journey called life. One cannot purchase, sell or pass down faith. It is internal and invisible.

Activating your faith

Faith is activated when it is unlocked. You unlock it when you are sick and tired or fed up with your current situation, circumstance or dissatisfied with the outcome of your life thus far. When insanity is too obvious and you want to change, your faith will be activated. One of my favorite illustrations about activating your faith is the story from Matthew 9:22, about the woman with the issue of blood. This woman suffered with continuous bleeding for 12 years. She heard Jesus was passing by. A crowd was surrounding Him. All of a sudden, Jesus asked his disciples "Who touched me?"

His disciplines thought this was a crazy question because there were so many people surrounding and touching Him. Jesus was actually referring to a person that had unlocked and activated her faith, a person who was sick and tired of being sick and tired and a person who wanted a future without bleeding, sickness, pain or ridicule, a person who reached out and put her faith with an action. Once again, this proves that, faith without works is dead. Not only did this lady believe, but she did something in addition to her belief. She activated her faith by touching the hem of his garment. Jesus was moved by this woman's faith.

Activate your faith and use it. Healing restoration, hope and rewards await you when you release your faith. God has given each of us a measure of faith. What we do or refuse to do with it will determine how high we rise or our destination's ending point. Faith is a promise from God. It is a mighty force, and should be used with extreme caution; because once you release your words and faith not even the sky can limit you. Internalize your faith. By faith we understand the world was formed. Faith that's tried and true helps us to get to the next level in our belief system.

Stepping in to the unknown

Faith is an effective method that has assisted me in destroying my fears. It is so much more that meets the eyes. Not only is faith a belief system, but it has the ability to help you step out of the past and into the present. Faith is hope in a brighter future and it is coming to a turning point, when you place your trust and hope in your Creator, surrendering to the Maker of the universe. Faith is a new beginning, filled with:

- no limits
- no boundaries
- no chains
- no shackles
- no gags
- no darkness
- no blinders

Faith is living life to the fullest, allowing God to work through you and fulfill the dreams and visons He has planned for you. In addition, faith is:

- walking in forgiveness
- speaking words into existence
- loving regardless of the cost
- stepping into the unknown with great expectations
- being optimistic in every situation
- looking up to the heavens and giving God thanks and knowing that He hears you loud and clear
- catching the vision, meditating on it and taking action

If you continue to live a life filled with fear, it will be virtually impossible to let much light in. You have to purpose in your heart that you refuse to be a victim any longer. Decide you will choose to live a life full of faith and hope. You will travel the road that is filled with faithfulness, goodness, hopefulness, and light. Proclaim you are no longer blinded by the work of darkness or your blemished past.

Fear is like a tightly closed fist. It is quite difficult for anything to pass through something that is closed. It would take much coaxing or forcing, similar to when fear is involved in your life. It is difficult to allow light into your life when fear is reigning supreme. Choose to open your hand. Release the stresses, expose the pain and scars. The fear will diminish and you will begin to heal. I am not implying that your past will vanish or you will become completely healed immediately. However, I am proclaiming that this is a start. Let's begin to move forward. Your life awaits you. Proclaim:

- I choose to take the road less traveled.
- I will not be bound by self-doubt or self-destruction.
- I will create the destiny I desire.
- I will fill my life with faith, love, hope and joy.
- I will be guided by my inner light.

Open your hands and your heart

Try this; stretch out one hand, palm up. As you can see, it is easier for something to pass through your open hand even sand and water can flow through when your hand is open. When you are open, you allow love, hope, peace, forgiveness and goodness to flow through your hands and heart. Know that change is never easy but usually necessary. Open our hands and heart. Let love and light in.

SECTION 3

Forgiveness

"I took a crucial step toward forgiving the killers that day. My anger was draining from me- I'd open my heart to God, and He'd touched it with His infinite love. For the first time, I pitted the killers. I asked God to forgive their sins and turn their souls toward His beautiful light".

Immaculee Ilibagiza

*F*orgiveness is such a beautiful gift. By far it is the greatest present you can give yourself. I strongly believe it's vital to our existence. I can attest that the power of forgiveness is life changing; it has changed my life and given me a new outlook. This wonderful act should be utilized liberally with no strings attached. Extending forgiveness as often as necessary will leave you with feelings of contentment and relief.

I have extended this gift to my offenders and it has literally saved my life. The hatred, strife, anger, pain, fears, bitterness, revenge, victim mentality and other negative thoughts they did not melt away instantly, however they left over time. The very act of forgiveness is not a onetime cure all, but it began the healing process and over time I experienced healing like never before. The famous saying, "time is a healer" definitely holds a lot of weight.

Healing and restoration is attainable, when realized, they will revitalize your life on many fronts. In fact, love and forgiveness are synonymous. There are countless verses in the Bible that talk about forgiveness, by far the most popular which can be recited by many around the world, John 3:16 reads, *"For God so loved the world, that he gave his only begotten Son that whosoever believeth in him should not perish, but have everlasting life."* It took this verse to transform my heart. I had so many negative things brewing within until I came to the realization that I was expected to forgive if I wanted the same in return. It was this turning point that caused me to change the course of my life.

Unforgiveness keeps you frozen in time. For countless years, I harbored it in my heart. I felt I had a viable cause to hold my offender captive. I relived haunting memories over and over with little relief. Little did I know, I was the only one carrying the grudge, resentments, suffering, pain and turmoil

44

on the inside. My offenders were living their lives as if nothing had taken place while I was trapped in my own self-imposed prison and I held the keys to my own freedom.

Releasing someone that has caused you harm or distress is not a onetime thing; however, you have the ability to free yourself from the bondage of unforgiveness. Not only is forgiving someone a sign of strength, but it is also liberating, somewhat akin to setting a prisoner free. There are many benefits associated with forgiving someone; the only person on the face of the earth that has the power to do it is the victim. Unlocking closed doors of your past and releasing the fears, pain, hurt, abuse, neglect, or whatever hardship you may have endured will yield great return. You have a choice; choose to free yourself no matter how painful it may seem to release the events that took place. You owe it to yourself to be restored to your original state of love and harmony.

Choose to forgive, not only will it make a world of difference, the extra weight will be lifted off your shoulders and life will never be the same. You will discover a newness and experience life in a whole new light when you choose to forgive. After all, it is not for your offender, rather it is for you. You deserve to be renewed, healed, restored and recovered from the past. Here is a list of some other benefits associated with forgiveness. They are generally positive in nature:

- mercy
- freedom
- cleansing
- love
- positivity
- fresh start

- rejuvenation
- recovery
- change
- hope
- wholeness
- releasing
- compassion
- helpfulness
- letting go

When you forgive someone it's as if you are detoxing yourself of the infection that has been eating at your very soul. Once again, forgiveness is a process. Long after you have extended the act, the thoughts, memories and events will resurface. They will revisit you when you least expect them, this is merely a test. The test is to see if you have truly been set free by the power of forgiveness. The hope is that when tested you will be able to prove to yourself that you have truly forgiven your offender. When the memories no longer have a hold on you and when you are not controlled by the past then you will know with great certainty that forgiveness has done its job.

Forgiveness helps you to get to the root of the issues that may be hindering your forward progress. Whatever seems to be hindering you, release it and know that your healing and restoration is waiting close by. The universe has sufficient healing elements to make you whole again. Time is the greatest healer, but you have to make a conscious effort to forgive.

Begin the healing process and let the forgiving virtues do the work in you. The act of forgiveness possesses the ability to:

- Sets you free
- Bring inner peace
- Restores hope
- Allows you to live again
- Gives you a way of escape
- Causes you to be optimistic
- Allows you to walk out of your past
- Leaves the past where it belongs 'in the past'
- Keeps the hurt, pain, abuse, and fears where they belong
- Opens new doors of possibilities
- Hopes for a bright future

I am certain of this one thing, love is supreme and in addition, forgiveness is the key to living a rich and fulfilling life, one without the fear of allowing your past to hinder your future. I can attest that there are many benefits to forgiving someone. An online article from greatergood.berkeley.edu (2016) explains, "Research over the past few decades has revealed enormous personal benefits to forgiveness" such as:

1. Forgiveness can make us happier.
2. Forgiveness improves our health.
3. Forgiveness sustains relationships.
4. Forgiveness is good for marriages.
5. Forgiveness boosts kindness and connectedness.
6. Forgiveness can heal the wounds of war.

While carrying around unforgiveness, I felt as though I was entitled to holding my offender captive. I was well beyond the state of bitterness. I allowed this cancerous disease to fester year after year, not realizing I had the power to put it at bay. I had the key to release myself from this death causing toxin, however it wasn't until I came to the realization that I had to forgive if I expected the same in return that I made a conscious effort to release the past and start afresh. No longer would I be controlled by my past and so I released it.

When you release yourself from the poison of unforgiveness you will feel new life flowing within your bones. Dispel the notion that trying to get back at your offender will solve what has already taken place. Vengeance is not yours, allow your Creator to deal with whomever has done you wrong. Refuse to continue wasting precious time scheming about how to get back at your wrong doers. They will have to give an account for the wrongs they have committed against you in due season. It's not your battle to fight or your problem.

I have come to know intimately that aside from love and forgiveness, time is the best healer. The universe is well able to take care of you, in fact, I dare to say, you will be reinstated with interest. Your time should be focused on healing and helping others to overcome what you have experienced rather than dwelling in the past.

What I'm about to say may sound cruel and heartless but the fact of the matter is, if you have been abused, neglected, done wrong or cheated in any way, shape or form it was for a reason. We don't always see the big picture when we are experiencing hardship but life is full of great lessons; some more painful than others. This may seem awkward but whatever you went through can now be a learning experience for others. Since you have lived it, you can tell it with great convictions.

The pain may have been temporary, but the memories may last a lifetime. Use your past hurt as a teacher. Use them to rise higher and help someone along the way. Refuse to be a victim, but rather a survivor. I reflect at the past hurt, pain, memories, rage, fears, nightmares and all of the negative thoughts associated with PTSD and I count myself thankful. Not for the PTSD itself but for the fact that I had the experience and now I can use it as a tool to help others who may be struggling with the same or similar battles. You can forgive and live a healthy life.

During the time I was living with unforgiveness, the events, pain, and memories followed me wherever I went. Regardless of how I tried to live a normal life they would show up without notice and stick around like an unwelcomed houseguest. It took many years to come to grips with myself. I finally came to the conclusion that if I expect to be forgiven, I too have to forgive others regardless of the wrong that was done against me. I forgave my abusers with my mouth but not with my heart. It wasn't until my heart changed that I noticed the burden was lifted off my shoulders.

Once again, restoration from unforgiveness did not happen overnight. As you are already aware, healing is a process, it takes time and there is not a specific set of time that signifies you are made whole. The pain did not disappear automatically. Unconsciously, I replayed the events constantly in my mind. I despised the memories and searched for healing year after year. Hopes of revenge were my only relief and comfort at times.

Other times, I didn't hope for amnesia but I wanted the events to disappear from my memory completely.

I am well aware of the great difficulties of not being able to erase or delete abuse, deception, or whatever hardship you endured. As the victim of a crime, the greatest gift you can give yourself is the gift of forgiveness. Forgiving your offender is a huge game changer because it's not for them but it's for you. It will make a world of difference. Moving on and overcoming unforgiveness is where the healing begins. You owe it to yourself.

I have known a beautiful lady for a number of years that harbored unforgiveness towards her ex-husband. On the surface she appeared normal. But the fact of the matter is she lived her live in a dark hole, she was numb and broken. She tried and tried day after day but she couldn't shake herself to move past her hurt, abandonment and betrayal. I encouraged her and hoped she would let it go, forgive and move on with her life. Of course it was easy for me to say because I did not know exactly what she was going through. Her pain was real and no doubt it affected her every waking hour.

A years later she still struggles with her divorce. It appears as if the betrayal has crippled her and depression is always knocking at her front door. I told her that what she experienced, no matter how painful it was, it was necessary to get her to this point in her life. I remind her that she was created for a specific reason and she is the only one on the face of the earth that can accomplish her mission. She along with every one of us has exactly what we need to overcome obstacles and fulfill our purpose in life.

I am sure my friend is not the only person struggling with this demon of unforgiveness. We all have our own individual prison. Isn't it time to break free? Remove the chains and shackles that have bound you for so long. Give yourself the gift of forgiveness. When you value yourself enough you will not allow anything to hinder you from *crushing your past, embracing your present and moving forward in the direction of your dreams*.

One of the most touching gesture of forgiveness I have read about occurred in the mist of the Rwandan Holocaust. Immaculee Ilibagiza, the author of _Left to Tell Discovering God Amidst the Rwandan Holocaust_, discovered the power of forgiveness despite the fact that hundreds of killers hunted for her day and night. She came to the realization that if she expected to be forgiven of her evil thoughts, she had to forgive the killers that were actively hunting for her as well. In like manner, if we desire to continue living on this planet, we must learn to live in forgiveness. It is ludicrous to expect forgiveness from the people we have done wrong, when we do not extend it ourselves.

Forgiveness is the most important thing you can do for yourself. It is the ultimate example of love. Love yourself enough by accepting your own forgiveness. Then your healing will begin to do its job. You have to release yourself from the past hurt, pain, abuse, failures, neglect or abandonment. Don't spend countless hours trying to figure it all out. Forgiveness is similar to a magical pill, like unto a healing medicine. When it is put in place it will make a world of difference. It will purify your heart and renew your mind.

Forgiveness yields many fruits; it will open invisible doors of new possibilities and allow you to witness things from a new point of view. Forgiveness is like unto a new born baby coming into the world. It is pure and unblemished by life's contaminations. Forgiveness is like healing for the soul. Once you get a taste of it, you will never be the same. When you forgive, your desire to return to that dark, dry, wretched and toxic place will no longer exist in your world.

Forgiveness is a powerful tool that leads to restoration; it is knocking at your heart's door. Look into the inner most depth of your heart and mind. There you will find contentment and a new sense of direction. You are worthy of your healing and restoration. Refuse to believe otherwise. There are many hidden truths buried deep down waiting to be revealed. You will be astonished when you take the time to zero in on your inner self. The answers to your questions lie within.

You have the ability to accomplish whatever you desire. Your true self is hidden beyond your clothes, façade, makeup and definitely your skin. Focus your attention internally and you will discover a greater level of contentment and inner peace. If someone has done you wrong forgive them. It will make a world of difference.

SECTION 4

Focus on your future

"*I was living proof of the power of prayer and positive thinking, which really are almost the same thing. God is the source of all positive energy, and prayer is the best way to tap in to His power*".
Immaculee Ilibagiza

*N*ow that we've looked at fear, faith and forgiveness it's time to focus on your future. Let's get ready for the preparation stage, which will include unlocking and activating your true self. After searching the inner most depth of your heart and mind, the hope is that you will discover where your inner strength lies.

Discovering what you are made of will lighten the load and may even give you the upper hand in this game called life. The strategies I have incorporated in this chapter will hopefully make the journey a little smoother. Prior to venturing on any journey, it is necessary to have some background knowledge of where you are headed, what route you will take and the amount of luggage that is allowed without paying any unnecessary baggage fee. Likewise, before beginning on your journey having a clear understanding of who resides on the inside of you is critical.

Your true or inner self must be one with your outer self. Knowing who you are and what you want to accomplish is paramount. As a matter of fact, knowing who you are is the first key to unlocking your destiny and walking in the direction of your dreams. For too long, I walked around in circles like a dog without a bone, going through the motions without being fulfilled. I lacked the tools needed, truth be told, not only was I extremely pessimistic but I also took everything at face value and usually foresaw the negative effect in most situations. Despite the fears that tried to control me, I knew deep within that I wasn't placed on this earth simply to take up space. I desired my time on this planet to be rich and fulfilling and so I took some proactive steps.

I discovered in order to truly get in tune with your true self you must take some private steps. No one should suspect what you are doing; your execution method will be based on personal preference. Like anything else worth having in this life it will take:

- Work
- Perseverance
- Discipline
- Self-monitoring
- Self-control
- Consistency
- Stamina
- Endurance
- Focus
- Determination

You will have to sacrifice your time and body to yield the results you desire. "No pain, no gain" should be your new motto if it is not already. Here are a few things that have proven effective for me. I hope they will assist you as well. I am not claiming this is the only route, however my upbringing, belief system and personal choice assisted in my decision-making. The seeds lying dormant within me merely needed watering. Praying, meditating and fasting have helped me discover a whole new world filled with unlimited possibilities. In fact, they were lifesaving to say the least.

In order to boldly walk in the direction of your dreams, you need to ensure you have prepared yourself for the uncertain journey. Begin one step at a time; start strong by having a plan of action. In addition, add to your list of essentials wisdom, patience and understanding. Here are a few strategies that I have utilized along the way and they have helped me tremendously.

Praying, meditating and fasting

Many may associate praying as a public gesture done by select religious officials for specific events such as funerals, weddings, religious services, inauguration ceremonies, graduations, public meetings or other gatherings. However, when you pray it should be a private act. No one should know what you are praying for, how long you are praying for or why you are praying except the One you are praying to. There will always be some controversy regarding how to pray, what to pray for, how long to pray and a plethora of other arguments. I am sharing what has been effective for me. There is no set order in which you have to execute these strategies.

Praying

More often than not, we pray as a last resort when our hands are tied, sometimes promising God "if He gets us out of this bind we will do certain things from hence forth." However, so many great things can occur when you take the time to be alone and communicate with your Creator. Truth of the matter is there is nothing fancy about praying, you do not need anything special aside from your lips and heart. Praying is a one-way communication between a person and a Deity. Simply speak to your God, Lord, Father, Yahweh, Jehovah, The Most High or whatever name you are accustomed to calling your Creator by.

- Most of us pray unknowingly on a daily basis, especially when faced with challenges or placed in difficult situations.

- Some of us perform rituals that must be followed to the tee such as a Third, Sixth and Ninth hour prayer.

- Some of us pray during the holiday especially at family gatherings, where the patriarch or matriarch sits or stands and says a prayer or blessing prior to eating.

- Some of us say a prayer before meals silently.

- Some treat praying as a lifestyle that is incorporated throughout the day.

- Some equate praying with breathing explaining the two are inseparable.

- All of us should make time to pray, for direction or guidance. Bottom line regardless of the route taken you should strive to pray.

A simple and effect way to communicate with your Higher Power is to find a quiet place where you can be alone. Connect with your Creator, greet Him with honor and respect for He is holy and higher than any earthly being. He is a spirit and He already knows everything about you. Don't be pushy. Humbly ask for direction and guidance and He will accept your petition. Ask Him to reveal the dreams He has placed within you. These dreams should line up with your gifts, hopes, aspiration, and desires. Be open and forthcoming and become vulnerable since He already knows everything about you. The most important thing you can do is pray about your:

- hurts
- fears
- pain

- past
- shame
- pride
- doubts
- hate
- sins
- anxieties
- forgiveness
- anything else that has the ability to hinder you from coming clean

Spill your guts if you will. Praying is similar to submitting or surrendering your all without fear or shame. The key is to let your feelings be known to the One who made you and brought you to this moment in time. You may cry, if and when you do that will be the start of something new. You may feel refreshed or renewed and that is a wonderful sign, the cleansing water of your tears is a reminder that you are indeed human.

Crying is not a sign of weakness; rather it is an acknowledgment that you are ready for a change to take place in your life. After you've cried your last tears, hopefully you'll feel a new sense of purpose. There are so many things or feelings that can take place when you take the time to be alone.

The fact of the matter is you should do what you need to communicate with your Higher Power. We all have a need to identify with our sense of purpose. Lay your hopes, dreams, and fears on the altar and leave them there. Become open and receptive. A relationship with your Creator takes place in your heart not in a building.

Praying does not necessary consist of long or drawn out words, phrases or sentences rather when you talk with your Creator, make your words be few. The heart is what truly holds the most weight not our words. Remember what you address Him by is not as important as the fact that you address Him with respect.

After you have finished laying your heart on the altar, in this case the altar I am referring to is a submitted heart not a physical one, but a spiritual one created by you. You will hopefully, be in a prepared state to listen to what your Creator has to tell you. Your spirit man is now ready to speak. Listen carefully; the quietness is the most intimate spot. Get there, pray and listen to what your inner man has to say to you.

Meditating

After you are finished speaking to your Creator, it will be His time to speak to and through you. When you become quiet, your inner self will speak to you. Some call it your spirit man, higher self, or true self while others call it your conscious self. Meditating is your time to focus on what you've asked for and for your Creator to give you information and or instruction. At this time, you simply close your mouth and open your mind. Allow your higher self or spirit to reveal things to you and lead you in the direction of your dreams. The spirit is gentle and will come when He feels invited. Here are a few keys that will help you shut off your outer and unlock your inner self:

- Unplug from technology
- Mute all unnecessary sounds, rings, dings, and alarms
- Find a comfortable place to sit

- Get comfortable
- Ensure your clothing is not constricting
- Cross your legs
- Place your lips together
- Open your mind

Shutting off your outer self will allow your inner self to rise up, speak up and reveal things to you, things that may have been dormant in your subconscious. There are numerous avenues to take when it comes to meditating. It will work if you work it. Ultimately, a quiet place and focus will help you unlock your true self. Meditating is not a one time or one shot thing. It takes practice, commitment and focus. If you are willing to unlock your inner self, you have to be comfortable. It can be challenging with our technologically driven lives however, it is possible to ignore the:

- rings
- dings
- binges
- alarms
- instant messages
- post status
- tweets
- other distracters

Make the effort, indeed it will pay off in the end. Searching for inner peace and direction will help you unlock sealed doors. Your inner self is waiting to embrace you. When you arrive at the place called silence, you will discover a quietness like never before. Whatever you decide to place your focus on should be brought front and center in your mind. Give full attention to it. Visualize yourself attaining that which you have placed in your focus and feel what it is like to have that which you hope for, already.

Remain in a state of concentrated focus. Your spirit man will show you many things you may have hoped, wished or thought about. You may see the answer to a question you struggled with. Your subconscious may even guide you in a new direction, revealing things that will take place in your future. Whatever the direction, know that this is a safe place one where the physical and the spiritual meets and communicates. Remain open and embrace the moment.

There may be tears, moans, groans or other sounds due to varying emotions. Fear not. The goal is to remain silent since there is little need for language in this awesome experience. The goal is to be caught up in the presence of silence and be surrounded completely with focus. You will see and hear with a new clarity like never before.

As you become more comfortable in your own skin, you may want to add breathing techniques, white sounds, candles, scents or anything else that may aid in creating a pleasant atmosphere. The desired outcome is to listen to your true self; the answers you are seeking are already available. You simply need to get quiet enough to hear. I love how Immaculee Ilibagiza puts it, *"When I meditated, I touched the source of my faith and strengthened the core of my soul."*

Fasting

A fast is not a diet, fad or public show. It's a private sacrifice between you and your Creator. Upon completion you should come to a new level of self-consciousness if you decide to abstain from certain foods and drinks. Ridding your body of the delicacies you enjoy is not an easy undertaking. However, with self-control and determination you can do it.

Think of something you enjoy and can't imagine doing without. Well a fast is when you deny yourself those things. There are a number of fasts that will help you rid your body of unhealthy toxins and possible excess weight. A quick search on the internet will present you with many options. Please be clear, a fast is not a diet. You are simply abstaining from certain foods such as sweets, animal byproducts, processed foods, and dairy for a set amount of time. The fact of the matter is fasting and meditating along with prayer can yield unimaginable results. At first this concept may seem like a huge undertaking but remember this is between you and your Creator. You are the director, you decide how and for how long you will fast or abstain from the foods you've decided on.

Similar to praying and meditating, fasting is a private thing. The primary difference is the fact that your body will be doing most of the work, but your mind and body will have to work together. There is no specific length of time to fast for, however it would be wise to come up with a plan and decide what works best for your lifestyle. Taking proactive steps will make the difference. If you are not familiar with fasting, once again there is a lot of option out there. The internet has loads of choices to pick from. *The Daniel Fast* has proven effective for me. However, it is a personal choice. When choosing a fasting program or route here are a few things you may want to consider abstaining from:

- Meats
- Dairy
- Liquor
- Artificial flavoring

- Yeast
- Anything that does not come directly from the earth (fruits, vegetables, and grains)

The primary focus of a fast is to rid your body of toxins and help it get back to its original state. Let me be clear, once again this is not a diet. Simply, it is a method to assist your body and mind to be in alignment. Some of the benefits will include:

- Weight loss
- Improvement in your overall health
- Balance
- Heightened senses
- Harmony

Incorporating praying, fasting and meditating into your life will yield great dividends. Aligning your heart, mind and body will give you a new outlook on life. The three separate entities working together will allow you to see with fresh eyes, listen with more clarity and appreciate life in itself. You will see things in a whole new light. Your senses may become more heightened because you have become more cognizant in mind, body and soul. Overall, you will be fueled and charged to begin your journey with a clear head, a healthier heart and on the right foot.

Drop the baggage

Obviously, I don't know what your dreams are and you may not have a clear picture of them at the moment either. However, make no mistake about it they are within you and they are within your reach. They have been lying dormant.

Here's the next step. Make a list of five things you have always wanted to accomplish, your dreams, hopes, desires or aspirations. Don't be timid and don't try to play it safe. Think big, the greater the dream, the greater the reward will be. It is your choice. No one will judge you. Regardless of how small or big jot them down:

1._____
2._____
3._____
4._____
5._____

A dream, desire, hope or aspiration is an activity that is expected to take place in the near or distant future. It has been placed in your heart and mind for a reason. You may have tried to dismiss them but they more than likely have grown roots. You may have tried to suppress them but they are too strong and alive to remain dormant. Others may have tried to destroy or suppress them; this is mere proof that they have taken root and is ready to be cultivated. Begin to make room so that it will have space to grow and multiply. It first begins with a belief in you. Self-confidence, unlike pride or boasting is essential since you will need them to carry you on your journey to fulfilling you dreams. Now let's get packing.

When you pray, fast and meditate focus on your list and visualize them as having been fulfilled. Continue to focus on them as long as necessary. There is no set time frame; you are ultimately the one who sets the pace. Remember nothing gets done until you do something and faith without works is dead. You have to take action.

Packing list

When going on a trip or a journey the preparation phase is essential. I have been on more trips than I can remember. The most challenging is always the packing stage. You have to be extremely selective in choosing what to pack. A basic packing list includes:

- personal hygiene items
- undergarments
- change of clothing
- footwear
- accessories
- identification and passport
- money
- other essential items

This list will generally take care of your needs if you pack wisely. In addition to the above items you should be as prepared mentally as possible because you never know when the unexpected may occur. Having too much luggage or baggage can be costly. You could lose precious time or money if you are not packed according to airline standards. On our most recent overseas trip, my husband and I traveled to Jamaica. As I was comparison shopping online for our tickets, I came across an airline advertising a rather competitive rate.

After reviewing their baggage rates and requirements, I soon discovered they were not included in the price of the ticket. In fact, they were al a carte at $50.00 per piece in addition to the ticket. I abandoned that site and continued my search for an all-inclusive flight. Upon arrival at the check in kiosk, I discovered I was only allowed two pieces but I had three. The airline's policy had recently changed however; the changes were not posted on the website. In an effort to avoid paying an additional cost, I suggested to my husband that we place our garment bag inside the suitcase.

Needless to say, we paid for an unexpected piece of luggage. So it is in life, policies can change without notice and sometimes we have to pay to carry around our excess baggage. Ensure you pack wisely; be conservative if you have to. Similar to traveling down this road called life, you should be certain you are equipped with the correct tools and resources needed to ensure success. Your duffle bag or suitcase should be light enough as to not cause you to stumble. Here are some things you should consider packing when going after your dreams, goals, hopes or aspirations:

- love
- peace
- faith
- understanding
- forgiveness
- hope
- pure heart
- joy
- gratitude
- compassion
- happiness
- focus
- determination
- self-control
- optimism
- grace
- inspiration
- selflessness

- contentment
- flexibility
- positivity
- peace
- kindness
- mercy

Now is the perfect time to do whatever you need to release the excess baggage out of your life. You will no longer have any need for the fearful past that tried to destroy you mentally, physically or emotionally. Get rid of your past for a brighter future. It's time to drop off the excess baggage, burn, destroy or abandon them at all cost. Dump the extra baggage, release your fears and drop the haters and doubters. Here are a few things you should consider abandoning prior to leaving for your journey:

- fear
- pride
- anger
- hate
- rage
- revenge
- strife
- envy
- wickedness
- unforgiveness
- fearfulness
- pain
- bitterness
- pessimism
- doubt
- blame
- anxiety

- self-hatred
- revenge
- hypocrisy
- violence
- negativity
- judgment
- hopelessness

Your bag should be filled with the above and anything else that will assist, motivate or help you get to your destination. No doubt your load may get heavy down the road, in fact, as you approach your destination of fulfilling your dreams your bag should be much heavier. It will be your job to share what you have attained along your journey to someone else. You should pass along your dreams to someone else so that they don't die. Whether it be a family member, friend or stranger is irrelevant as long as you pay it forward.

We are placed on this planet for a short time and we should strive to make a difference regardless of how small it may seem to us. We need people to continue the circle of life. However, there will no doubt be some that will not have your best interest at heart. Get your head and heart focused on the finished line. This is your race no one can run it for you. Leave your past where it belongs as well as anyone who tries to hinder you. Dump the extra baggage, release your fears and drop the haters and doubters. You will be able to see clearly and begin on the right foot:

- Let love lead you
- Position yourself to win
- Lighten your load
- Forgive and forget

- Surrender to your Creator
- Start off with a fresh outlook on life
- Believe you will accomplish all you put your head and mind to

Get ready

Get your mind right, your destiny awaits. Get in the game; you will notice a dramatic change in your life and overall outlook. Purpose, focus and determination are the keys. You can stand firm without any doubts or misconceptions about your destination or outcome. Look yourself in the mirror and affirm the following:

- I am bold
- I am fearless
- I am focused
- I am determined
- I am strong
- I am powerful
- I am optimistic
- I am flexible
- I am forward looking
- I welcome change in my life

When you get to your destination, your bag should be full. You should not only gain new insights and experiences, but you should be ready, willing and able to hand over what you have attained to someone else, pay it forward. We should strive to make a difference in our daily lives.

Get ready for the ride of your life. Take inventory and keep only the necessities. Everything else is excess baggage.

Yes, the journey will be exciting. Remember to stay open to change knowing that it is not always easy but it's usually necessary to move you from your stagnant position and propel you into your destiny. Remain optimistic, expect great things to take place in your life and they will. Tap into your true self and know that whatever you need is available to you. Allow the universe to work for you and you will be surprised at the manifestation of the things you hope and wish for.

SECTION 5

Let the journey begin

"But I came to learn that God never shows us something we aren't ready to understand. Instead, He lets us see what we need to see, when we need to see it. He'll wait until our eyes and heart are open to Him, and when we're ready, He will plant our feet in the path that's best for us...but it's up to us to do the walking," Immaculee Ilibagiza

*A*s with any new endeavor, your journey will not be a walk in the park. Without a doubt, there will be hindrances, roadblocks, dead ends, U-turns and all sort of other obstacles. Plan accordingly, do your due diligence. Researching the next phase and doing some ground work will prove extremely helpful in the end. On the journey to fulfilling your dreams, the road will have many twist, turns and uncertainties. No doubt you will:

- get lonely at times
- feel like quitting
- slip, slide, trip or fall
- get stuck in the mud
- feel frozen at times

Regardless of what may appear in front of you, don't be ruled by your feelings or emotions. Whatever you decide, stick with it until the end. Worry not as to how long things are taking to come to fruition. Embrace your journey, regardless of how rocky the road may seem; your rewards can be attained at the end of the race. Know that small risks equate to small rewards whereas, big risks equal bigger rewards.

When you decided to take that leap of faith, be forewarned. There will be a constant pull to the left insisting that you come back to what is safe, normal or comfortable. Remain focused on the future and know that this feeling is merely a distraction. Continue moving forward, do not waiver to the left or the right. The enemy of your soul is trying to sabotage your dreams and steal your future. Don't allow his schemes to divert you. Regardless of the test you can pass it. Fix your eyes forward, you are stronger than you think, you have super natural strength, look within and activate it.

Getting your hands dirty is a sure sign of progress. Dirty hands prove that work is in full effect. In order for your dreams to come to completion you have to work them. Don't think for a moment that the journey will be a walk in the park. You will encounter your fair share of:

- naysayers
- stumbling blocks
- traps
- doubters
- bumps in the road
- dead ends
- detours
- delays
- opposing invisible forces
- rough terrains

Fear not, stay the course and keep your eyes fixed on the direction and destination of your dreams. Unlock the power that's lying inside. This is your time, if you must; saturate yourself with hope, faith, love and forgiveness. All of which come from within. These invisible gifts grow when they are watered similar to a natural plant. Whatever your gifts are, they will help propel you to a higher level and take you before great men, however you must cultivate, prune and give them time and space to grow. Bottom line, to reap a harvest you must do the work. The sooner you choose to commit and submit the faster you will yield your harvest.

- Commit to love.
- Commit to harmony.
- Commit to excellence.
- Commit to forgiveness.

- Commit to your dreams.
- Commit to your family.
- Submit to your spouse.
- Submit to your parents.
- Submit to you elders.
- Submit to your superiors.

Every second that ticks by we are either changing, or wondering why things are changing around us. With that being said we must make a conscious effort to self-evaluate our word choices and decision-making process. When you walk in the direction of your dreams you must remain conscious and alert because fear will attempt to creep in unsuspectingly and deter you. Be vigilant and stay the course. If you see something lacking, be an agent of change and change it. We are all consumers of other people's dreams, someone did the ground work and we now benefit from something that was simply an idea. Just about everything you see and use in the natural world came from someone's mind and hard work. Take for instance:

- The builder of the home you reside in had an idea to build a house.

- The manufacturer of the vehicle you drive had an idea to build a vehicle.

- The farmer of the foods you eat had an idea to plant the seeds.

- The designer of the bed you sleep in had an idea to manufacture the bed.

- The designer of the clothes you wear had an idea to sew fabrics together.

- The creator of the phone you use had an idea to create an easier way to communicate.

- The creator of the technology you can't live without had an idea to make our lives more progressive.

- The creator of the internet had an idea to connect the world.

- The creator of social media had an idea of how to socialize the globe without traveling.

This proves once again that we are all physical creators. You possess the ability to create the life you desire. What dream will you fulfill? What legacy will you leave when your spirit departs your mortal body? Now it's your time to turn your dreams into reality.

Revisit your list of five most pressing things you wish to accomplish. Take note of them and take action. Every step you take is a learning experience regardless of how painful it may be. Some steps will be safe like a walk in the park, while others will be downright scary. Regardless, you must continue fearlessly. Each of your steps has been approved by your Creator. You must believe He has your best interest at heart. He confirms this in his word that you are the "apple of his eyes." Your outward appearance does not play a significant role in the grand scheme of things. Your intestinal fortitude is much more important. Refuse to hold on to anything too dearly in this life because it's all fading away; therefore, do what needs to be done while you have the time. We are all vessels, waiting to be poured out. What will you release when your time comes? You can only pour out what you are filled with, will it be:

- Love
- Hope
- Encouragement
- Peace
- Hatred
- Envy
- Strife
- Fear
- Contention

Fill yourself with love, purity, and goodness because whatever you sow that shall you also reap. What is the biggest thing that has changed in your life? Is it your mind or way of thinking? The hope is that both has undergone a transformation. Of course the physical change is obvious, but the change with the most impact is your knowledge of yourself and the world around you. How you react to situations and the way you treat others make the greatest impact. It is during the most trying times you will discover a personal change.

I am love because God is love. I am a creator because my Creator fashioned me so that I might create as well. I create by speaking life into existence. You create by using your words and speaking whatever you desire into existence. You have the ability to watch your words manifest into something tangible, affirm:

- I am smart, worthy and valuable.

- I will not stop until I achieve a higher level of consciousness.

- I will give every fiber of my being to ensure I fulfill my dreams.

- I choose to allow only positive and radiant energy into my life.

- My goals are within reach; I will not quit, retreat or surrender.

Initiative

Take a quick look at the word initiative. You will notice the beginning from which we get the word initial. Initial is the beginning of something. In order to accomplish anything in life you have to take the initial step. This is called taking action. Initiative similar to faith, love and forgiveness can't be bought; rather they are internal. Nothing great can truly be accomplished without intestinal fortitude. Initiative is a driving force that can propel you into the future.

Take the initiative, start on your journey, successful people recognize the importance of this very truth. Nothing can be done if nothing is begun. You have to do something in order to get something.

No one can make you start on your dreams. I can ask, challenge, beg, or inspire you to begin. However, you must take the initiative. It has to begin internally not externally. You have to want to accomplish or realize your dreams in order for them to be realized. You already have everything you need within you to succeed. You are equipped with all the tools needed to win in this life. We are spiritual beings living in a mortal body. Everything we need is available within. We merely need to be challenged, encouraged, supported or guided. Love is the ultimate healer. In addition, I would include forgiveness, time and a change in mindset. They will elevate any situation and help you get to that place of healing, contentment and inner peace.

It will take stamina and endurance to make it to the end

Stay the course, regardless of how uncomfortable you may get. Know that there's always a light at the end of the tunnel.

There will be difficulties, challenges, second guessing and an endless list of what "ifs". Regardless, you must continue to press forward. This life is filled with uncertainties. Make it your priority to plan the outcome you desire. You and only you can control your choices. Your actions or lack thereof will dictate your outcome.

Whatever you do, don't lose heart. Be your greatest cheerleader. You have to continue fighting, the finish line is within reach, and you have everything needed to win the race. Be reminded that you are not alone. Help is always a call or click away. With the abundance of information out there, you can find encouragement somewhere. Inspiration is all around. Continue the fight; yes, your race will call for a few battles here and there. Know that you are equipped with the strength you need. Keep going; remember you can't win unless you fight. Get your head in the game and don't give up. If you can't find a way, make a way. No one else can perform the work you were destined to do. You are in charge of your destiny. Every lesson learned will be useful for the next step.

Abandoning your past

One of the most difficult things to do is leaving the past where it belongs, in the "past" of course. Aside from allowing unforgiveness to fester in your bones, living in regret comes in at a narrow second. I implore you to refuse to continue living a life filled with unnecessary pain this very instant. Resist the need to be held captive by your past hurt, pain, regrets, what ifs, could haves, should haves, would haves, etc. It is unhealthy, unproductive and serves no purpose under the sun. Give yourself permission to abandon your past, regardless of how painful, difficult or unpleasant it may be. You must take this vital step in order to embrace your present.

Life is intended to be lived in the here and now. No need to continuously revisit your dark past. The challenges or obstacles you experienced have served their purpose. Indeed, use them as refining tools. Learn from them and allow them to be your fertilizer. Grow, blossom and bloom into the amazing person you were created to be. Your future is illuminating with light and love. Indeed, it is astounding, grab hold of it. This hope for a brighter future is a vital step in your new life. Take it by the horn and hold on for the ride of your life. It will pay great dividends in the end. Let it count. You have so much ahead as opposed to what you experienced in your past.

No doubt that there will be challenges and obstacles ahead. No worries. You are equipped with the necessary tools needed to succeed and exceed your own expectations. Look within for guidance and direction. You will be amazed at your internal strength. If you knew the power that lies within the human mind and heart, you would be astoundingly flabbergasted.

Purpose

Dr. Wayne Dyer explains, *"Once you place a thought into your imagination about who you want to become, I encourage you to live from that end as if it had already materialized into the physical realm."* Contrary to popular belief, our life's purpose is not merely to leave an earthly legacy for future generations. Rather, it is to fulfill our calling. We are all sent into this world on a specific assignment for a period of time. It is our responsibility to do our due diligence and discover why we were chosen to tread upon this earth. Whether it is to teach, sing, preach, dance, lead, write, motivate or simply lighten the load of the down trodden, you are the only one that can truly answer the age old questions, "Why am I here?" and "What is my purpose on this earth?" Both of which have baffled millions. Searching high or low externally will not give you the answers to life's most sought after questions. In fact, it will leave you with a void that can never be filled. From the creation of mankind, there have been countless numbers of wandering souls who have traveled this earth and left without unlocking the door that held the keys to their life's purpose. *Knowledge by itself is useless until you internalize and apply it.*

Many of us spend our entire lives living in a box. Most dare not embrace this magnificent, living, breathing universe. Our closed mindedness has caused us to miss many life-changing opportunities, ones which may have well helped countless lives on our travel down this road called life. I implore you; refuse to continue living in your self-imposed microcosmic world. Now is the time to discover all this beautiful world has to share with you. Because all creation derives from the imagine and likeness of the Creator, we are all a reflection of Him. We ought to take heed and stop limiting Him.

Throughout the four corners of this world, we can witness His greatness. Therefore, we should do the same. We should embrace all people and respect their culture including their choice of worship. Doing so will open our eyes and hopefully cause us to see this world in a new light. Dismiss the need to continue judging others based on the tone of their skin, national origin, gender, ethnicity, or any other external factors. As human beings, we cannot change where we originate from and hence should not be discriminated against by such a minimal thing. We ought to take a good look at how we separate humanity for no viable reason except in the name of religion.

SECTION 6

Keys to overcoming obstacles

"Our losses and setbacks provide lessons and opportunities for us to live more fulfilled and grateful lives. Like gold, we are purified and made better by going through the fires in our lives."
Aya Fubara Eneli

*O*bstacles, detours, trials, hold ups and setbacks appear in our lives to help build our characters. They are inevitable, if we could avoid them, we surely would. Regardless of their sizes, shapes, or colors; you have everything you need on the inside to overcome them. You may have to face some rugged, rough, sandy, muddy or rocky roads on your journey. Don't focus on the terrain. Look at them as a smooth path waiting to be trod upon. U-turns are allowed on your path and road blocks are placed on your path to test your tolerance and patience level.

Remain in control of your emotions since blaming yourself or others will only make matters worse. Self-discipline is a sure sign of maturity therefore, harness your inner energy on problem solving and remain focused. Never allow your situation to define you or get the best of you. Rather remain optimistic, open and flexible. Restraint is a great tool that should be utilized during uncertain times. Overcoming obstacles helps you to build a tough outer shell plus when you have overcome enough obstacles you will be able to guide someone in the right direction, thanks to your experience.

Win whatever the cost. Always remember you are in control. Nothing can happen to you without your permission. Never allow situations and things to define you; rather you define them. Jump over those obstacles, fight and win at this game called life.

It only takes one situation to change your life

Life is such a journey filled with unpredictability around every corner. One day you could be "sitting on top of the world" or on the 24th floor in a resort admiring the view and contemplating the future. While the next day you could be stuck in the sand on an unmanned road in the middle of the desert attempting to locate where you are without the help of technology; simply because you made one wrong turn. Let me share a quick story of how I came to experience firsthand what is truly meant by the statement, "obstacles are character builders".

My family and I were 2000 miles away from home. We were traveling on a graveled dirt road. Our navigation had always guided us in the past. So no big deal, we had no reason to doubt it wouldn't continue to do its job. We were driving for what seemed like 20 miles. The navigation kept on refreshing to find a new route; it does that in instances when the road is unfamiliar.

Needless to say, we continued on our journey through the dry, mountainous and deserted land. All of a sudden the dirt road turned into a sandy road. As we continued on our journey we had to go around a steep hill since the highway was a few miles up the road. My husband was maneuvering our truck meticulously, because we were sliding a little. Unfortunately, our two wheeled drive truck was no match for the sand. We were stuck in the middle of no man's land. The only sign of life was a cow we saw about ten miles earlier. We exited the vehicle and assessed the situation.

It appeared as if our rear tires were two feet in the sand and the vehicle would not budge. We attempted to use our cell phones to contact our roadside assistance, but we could not get any service. My husband began to walk around in an attempt to pick up a signal from a cell phone tower, after about a half a mile he was able to find a signal. He was informed by our roadside assistance that they could not assist us because we were too far off a paved road. Ordinarily, I would have been furious, but not this time. Not only was I cool as a cucumber, but I felt this peace come over me like never before. It was during this difficult and uncertain time that I realized my change had manifested itself. I was in control of my thoughts and actions. Not only was I leaping for joy on the inside, but I couldn't wipe the smile off my face.

My husband returned to the truck and decided we would have to solve this problem, since help was not on the way. After collecting a few rocks and some wood and placing them under the tires we were able to get the truck out of the sand and continue on our way.

About a quarter of a mile down the road, we got stuck again; as we attempted to go up what appeared to be a huge mount. This time we were really stuck and the only call we could make was an emergency call, after we picked up a signal. My husband was able to get in contact with the county sheriff. There was no landmark, or signs to assist us but he used his military navigation skills and was able to give the coordinates to the Sheriff's department. The fact of the matter is the only thing I saw was mountains and sand dunes.

We were informed that our rescue was placed on hold because the department had to tend to a life threatening emergency. We continued to problem solve since we did not know if and when the Sheriff department would locate us. Once again, we placed rocks, woods, clothes, brush and anything we could find under the tires; unfortunately, we only sank deeper in the sand. We accepted the fact that we probably would have to sleep in the truck until the next day if we could not be rescued.

After about five hours we heard someone yelling, it was the Sheriff's department. The officer parked about half a mile away because he did not want to risk getting stuck in the sand as well. What a sigh of relief, we were rescued right at sundown. The sky was breathtaking and I really had a reason to be thankful.

What an experience riding in the back of a police SUV, talk about a bumpy ride. It was now fully dark and maneuvering our way out of the rugged terrain proved to be a challenge. It seemed as if we were on an African safari. The seat in the vehicle was uncomfortable to say the least. The sergeant was extremely kind, and he kept apologizing for all the bumps in the road. It wasn't his fault; we were all experiencing the same ride even though our heads hit the roof of the SUV a few times because of the rugged terrain. We made a few wrong turns and the sergeant said we may need to be rescued again since he was not familiar with this part of the mountain. After much driving, about two hours, we made it to the main road. We were overcome with joy. The first hotel the sergeant brought us to was booked, but thankfully the second one had rooms available.

Early the next day we attempted to get a tow company that would agree to tow our vehicle out of the sand. The two youngest children and I stayed in the hotel while my husband and eldest son went with the tow truck driver to retrieve our truck. The kids and I spent time praying, reading and writing. I was engrossed in writing the above paragraph when I checked the time. We had less than 15 minutes to check out of the hotel. As soon as I said let's get ready to leave, I received a text from my husband stating, "We have the truck, we're on the way back."

Talk about happy, the kids began to celebrate as well. With nine minutes to spear we gathered our belongings and prepared to check out of the hotel. We were not only very thankful that we had been rescued, our vehicle was recovered, but we also received a 50% discount off our tow bill.

We remained optimistic and had confidence that everything would work out as planned. We expected the removal of our truck from the sand, prayed, meditated and spoke positive words about our situation into the universe and left the rest up to God. I was reminded of the scripture, *"He will never give you more than you are able to bear."* I am extremely grateful that we were able to get out of Winnemucca, NV before the snowstorm hit. Prayer and focus definitely worked. This experience will forever be in my heart.

By far that was a challenging situation, one in which I found out that you should never allow your situation to control you rather control yourself. It was during this uncertain time, I felt the most peace, a sense of calmness like I had never felt before. I focused on the outcome rather than the problem. I chose to visualize the problem as solved and was overjoyed within because I knew everything was working for my good.

When faced with an obstacle or problem rest assured that you too can have the same assurance that things will work out in your favor. Remain optimistic, keep your composure and stay focused on the solution.

Lessons learned: Do not go looking for battles to fight, they will find you. When they do you will be tried. Be certain to stay focused. Do not waiver to the left or the right, rather:

- remain calm
- look up

- call out for help
- send up a silent prayer
- remain in a state of gratitude

Remember you reap what you sow. Remain full of faith and believe the universe is working on your behalf.

Trials, obstacles, setbacks, U-turns, roadblocks and hindrances are opportunities to rise up and demonstrate your true character. These character builders are great tools to test your faith and produce patience. Your true character will be magnified when you are tested. Fear not! This is your time to shine when your faith is under fire; the ultimate outcome you hope to accomplish is patience and discipline. Whatever you're made of will reveal itself when you are tested and tried. Trust God and believe He shall direct your path. Focus not on the situation, but on the outcome.

SECTION 7

Inspiration

"God and Nature first made us what we are, and then out of our own created genius we make ourselves what we want to be. Follow always that great law. Let the sky and God be our limit and Eternity our measurement." *Marcus Garvey*

*I*nspiration evokes a special emotion when activated. It's that special feeling you get that causes your senses and emotions to spark immediately. Inspiration is everywhere; take a 360 degrees glance around. You will find it at home, in nature, in the big things and even in the mundane. Take the time to observe and listen to life as it happens, you will be inspired. When you are open to love, peace, harmony and tranquility you will experience life to the upmost. Look up at the sky; the clouds shield the sun when the earth gets too hot. The rain descends and refreshes the earth; the snow falls and creates blankets of whiteness in its season.

All the wonderful things that heaven gives us are indeed free gifts, don't take it for granted; rather appreciate the beauty that comes down from above. Inspiration not only descends from above but it may just be staring you in the eyeballs. Become one with your environment, inhale and embrace each moment. Let your senses go wild. Be in the moment; refuse to let it pass you by. Regardless of where you live or work, immerse yourself in the moment. You may be working in a school, warehouse, office, toll booth, truck, house, coal mine, store, hospital, church, prison or elsewhere, it matters not. Embrace each moment; don't' let your life pass you by:

- Don't take another moment for granted.
- Tomorrow is not promised.
- Live your life to the fullest.

Listen to the sounds of love, hope and perfection. The children, animals, birds, wind, and best of all the sound of nothingness. How beautiful, the simple sound of silence. It is in this quiet time I feel more alive than any other moment.

Quiet down and become one with your inner man. He's calling, yelling, screaming to speak with you. "Will you make time for Me?" I have so much to share with you. I implore you, give me your ears.

Come, listen.
I desire to share the secrets of life with you.
Make yourself available.
I want to sing sweet songs like none you've heard before.
I want and desire to be with the one I love and know so well.
Come, let's connect.
Please, I want to talk with you, but not just when you lie down in the wee hours of the night when you are resting.
Make time for me in the day as well.
I know you're afraid of the quietness.
Why?
What have I done but waited patiently for you?
Unplug because you are consumed by noise.
Noise is here, there, everywhere,
too much noise that clouds your ability to think clearly.
Listen to the children's laughter.
Does it remind you of a dream or a sweet childhood memory?
The innocence, remember when?
Return to your first love.
I'm here just watching and waiting, waiting for you.

Nature is calling

The trees are waiting to dance for you. Go ahead walk bare foot on the soil and the dirt; I believe it's got healing power waiting to make you whole again. The birds are ready to sing for you. The water is ready to purify and heal you. The animals are waiting to warn and direct you. The children are ready to play for you.

The sun is waiting to shine and warm your heart. The moon is ready to light your path. What are you waiting on? Time is slipping by. Don't live from a factory or a box. Plant a garden. Eat a fruit, feed the ducks, climb a tree better yet a mountain.

Close your eyes, inspiration is everywhere. It's internal as well as external. Choose to be inspired, for beauty is in the eyes of the beholder. You can choose to be touched by nature or better yet, touch nature with your presence. This vast universe holds the key to your contentment. Step outside, use your senses and embrace your surroundings. Whatever situation you are placed in, be certain you can find inspiration if you look far or wide. No matter how dim it may appear, be thankful and smile at the world because the world is smiling at you.

SECTION 8

Putting it all together

"God sent me on earth. He send me to do something, and nobody can stop me. If God want to stop me, then I stop. Man never can. "
Bob Marley

If you are waiting for the perfect moment to start on your dreams, goals or aspirations, hang it up! This should come as no surprise, but the perfect moment will never come. Seriously it doesn't exist; there will always be an abundance of excuses which will appear more important the instant you attempt to start. In order to get the ball rolling you have to start. Take the initiative, make up your mind now, the decisions you make or not will affect you and your future.

Quick question, when you come to the end of your life will it be full of regrets or memories of the wonderful experiences you created and lived out? Regardless of the price, are you willing to pay it? Irrespective of the situation, you have to demand change if you truly desire it. Do something different, change your mind, only then will you make forward progress. When you've tried and failed, don't quit. Never allow your situation to define you, it is merely temporary. If all else fails, throw up the universal signal of surrender, submit your all to your Creator. He knows you intimately, since He fashioned you in His image and likeness and placed your dreams within you. He wants you to prosper, live out your dreams and make your mark on this earth. Take the leap of faith and move forward.

Procrastination

If you've made it this far in this book, then you are serious about going after your dreams. Thank you for your commitment to changing your outlook on life. Procrastination is the greatest factor to unfilled dreams, remember, nothing started equates to nothing completed. As I've stressed, there will never be a perfect time to begin, initiate now. My ultimate goal is not to sway you to the left or the right. Rather it is to present a choice to you. It is to challenge you to do what you have always dreamed of doing. Go after your dreams! Of course the road may get rocky, bumpy or uncertain; there may be some U-turns or even dead ends. Fear not! Everything you need is available on the inside. You have the tools and resources needed to succeed. Look down deep into the inner most part of your heart, search your mind, the universe is willing and waiting to assist you. Allow good things into your life. ***Whatever you allow will show up when you least expect it.*** Words of caution; be prepared, because the moment you release your words they have the ability to manifest themselves immediately.

Nothing but a number

Age is nothing but a number. Regardless of the number of years you've been on this earth, you are well able to accomplish your dreams and goals. The formula is the same across the board. Yes, some tweaking may be required but if you are persistent and focused you can reap the rewards. Wherever you are in life at this moment isn't as important as where you are heading. You can change your location or surroundings, but most importantly, you have to change your mind otherwise things will remain the same. When you unlock your true self, you will discover a new world filled with new possibilities. You are not a loser because you lose a race. That was merely one race. Get up, get back to training camp and find another race to run. With the right environment, support and resources you can win. Your experience is unique to you and that's what makes you so special to this universe.

The Challenge

- I challenge you to take the first step to a brighter future.
- I challenge you to move out of your comfort zone.
- I challenge you to always spread love.
- I challenge you to walk in peace.
- I challenge you to walk in forgiveness.
- I challenge you to change your perspective.
- I challenge you to allow your intuition to guide you.
- I challenge you to combine your faith with works.
- I challenge you to live life to the fullest

In closing

I challenge you to search deep within your inner most being. All you need to fulfill your hopes and dreams is within reach:

- Recognize your fears and overcome them.
- Activate your faith.
- Walk in forgiveness.
- Pray, meditate, fast and prepare for the journey of your life.
- Get your mind in focus.
- Take only what is necessary.
- Embrace obstacles and use them as character builders.
- Look for inspiration in everything.
- You are in control of your destiny.

Your journey will be based on the decisions you make right now.

- Take the initiative.
- Make your move and remain focused
- Continue to learn.
- Remain open to change
- Control your emotions.
- Do not allow your emotions to get the best of you.
- You can accomplish whatever you place your focus on.

You may not be able to immediately change your job, housing, or other external things. However, change the things you are able to change and head in the direction of your dreams. As I've stated in section one:

"Buried alive and completely useless are many possibly world changing and life altering ideas that have been locked away in an unrecoverable black box of dream killing fear. If the graves could release their secrets, they could reveal many inventions that had the possibility to change the course of history by improving life on earth, curing deadly diseases, or discovering ways to improve our planet. The possibilities were endless."

Don't die with your dream in you. Your mission on this planet is to realize your dreams, overcome obstacles and experience this life to the utmost. Start today. Malcom X puts it this way: *"The future belongs to those who prepare for it today."*

Keep it going

Here are some techniques you may want to consider incorporating in your daily lifestyle:

- Pray--surrender to your Creator. Thank Him for His unconditional love and ask Him for guidance and direction.
- Meditate--wait on your Spirit man to speak to you. Listen and take action.
- Speak positive things into your life.
- Look for ways to lend a helping hand.
- Be inspired by your environment.

Share your story, thoughts and questions with me. Visit my group page on Facebook (**the opposite of fear is faith**).

BIBLIOGRAPHY

Banaszak, Doreen. *Excuse Me, Your Life is Now: Mastering the Law of attraction.* Hampton Roads Publishing. Charlottesville, VA: 2007.

Bodo, Murry. *Through the Year with Francis of Assisi: Daily Meditations from His Words and Life.* Image Books. New York: 1987.

"CDC-Carbon Monoxide Poisoning- Frequently Asked Questions." (10 February 2015). Accessed March 20, 2016. cdc.gov/co/faq.htm

Dyer, Wayne W. *Wishes Fulfilled: Mastering the Art of Manifesting.* Hay House. Carlsbad, CA: 2012.

Eneli, Aya Fubara. *Live Your Abundant Life: Encouragement and Strategies to Create a Meaningful and Fulfilled Life.* Xulon Press: 2004.

What is Forgiveness? Accessed July 1, 2016. www.greatergood.berkeley.edu/topic/forgiveness/definition

Ilibagiza, Immaculee. *Left To Tell: Discovering God Amidst the Rwandan Holocaust.* Hay House. Carlsbad, CA: 2014.

PTSD: National Center for PTSD. Accessed July 18, 2016. http://www.ptsd.va.gov/public/PTSD-overview/basics/what-is-ptsd.a

ABOUT THE AUTHOR

Joan E. Ruffins, a native of the island of Jamaica, is the wife of Lawrence and the mother of Tre, Javon and Lauren. She is a minister, Veteran, educator and speaker. Joan has a heart for people and is passionate about teaching. She earned her Master's Degree in Leadership from Grand Canyon University, Bachelor's Degree in General Studies from Excelsior College and her Associate Degree in Political Science from Broward Community College. Joan has traveled the lower 48 states, and five countries. She enjoys taking pictures, painting, reading and writing. Her passion is encouraging and challenging others to embrace this magnificent life and go after their dreams, regardless of the cost.

To contact Joan for one-on-one coaching or inquire about group presentations, please e-mail her at
authorjoanruffins@gmail.com

Follow her on:
Twitter:@joanruffins
Instagram:@jeruffins
Facebook:@authorjoanruffins

Mail may be sent to:
P.O. Box 895196
Leesburg, FL 34789-5196

Notes

Notes

Notes

Made in the USA
Columbia, SC
02 March 2019